Ms. Jennifer V. Matthews is a Library Media Specialist for the Mt. Vernon City School District. She is a member of the Academy of American Poets, the American Library Association, and the United Federation of Teachers. She has won the Alice Minnie Heniger Award for the best work of literature for Children from Lehman College (City University of New York) in May 2003. Ms. Matthews has a Master of Science degree in Literacy from Alfred University. This is her first poetry book.

For a

GHETTO CHILD

Jennifer V. Matthews

AUSTIN MACAULEY PUBLISHERS™

LONDON • CAMBRIDGE • NEW YORK • SHARJAH

Copyright © Jennifer V. Matthews (2019)

Ordering Information:
Quantity sales: special discounts are available on quantity purchases by corporations, associations, and others. For details, contact the publisher at the address below.

Matthews, Jennifer V.
For a Ghetto Child

ISBN 9781641825399 (Paperback)
ISBN 9781641825405 (Hardback)
ISBN 9781645364405 (ePub e-book)

Library of Congress Control Number: 2019937262

The main category of the book — JUVENILE NONFICTION / Poetry / General

www.austinmacauley.com/us

First Published (2019)
Austin Macauley Publishers LLC
40 Wall Street, 28th Floor
New York, NY 10005
USA

mail-usa@austinmacauley.com
+1 (646) 5125767

This book is dedicated with love to the children at P.S. 49.

To Ingrid Menendez

Studio in a school

Your insight, thoughtfulness, and honest opinion of my work paved the way to a wealth of ideas. Thank you.

A special thanks to Irina Delof and Larnie Fox, who gave me the permission to use their artwork in this anthology. I owe you both more than words can convey.

I am also appreciative of Brian Owens, who gave me the permission to use his father's works.

Many thanks to the award-winning illustrator, Bryan Collier, who gave me the permission to use his paintings. They are featured on pages 19, 28, and 31.

The Hummingbird by Irina Delof

Jamila's Surprise by Carl Owens

Burn by Larnie Fox

White Magnolia by Irina Delof

The Flower by Irina Delof

The Swan by Irina Delof

Celestial Sisters by Carl Owens

Children of Eden by Carl Owens

Girl Talk by Carl Owens

Contents

Hopes

Hope

Hope is a seashell lying on the sand

Waiting to be discovered

Alone with the White Sand

White sand trickling through my fingers

Falling on the sandy shore

The strong breeze blowing the sand away

Scattering salty grains all over the earth

Then there comes the rain

One drop, two drops

Frothy waves riding the high wind

Touching my bare feet

Tickling...

I hear a clap of thunder

And I see the lightning flash

Then I look up and I see

The cloudy sky

And I remember

I am alone with the

White sand...

The Flower

A flower whispered

And under that

I found my song

For a Ghetto Child

It is the cold time my love

A time when the bullets pierce

The hearts of our young ones

A time when the rain

Walks with us wherever we go

And little children

Bow their heads in anger and sorrow

And ask

Where is the tomorrow?

The little white birds that've come out to play

Have gone to find a place to stay

Leaving empty streets

And hanged their heads on their breasts

And allow the bullets to sing

For there is no joy in the ghetto, my love

No warmth

Just a bullet in the heart of a red rose

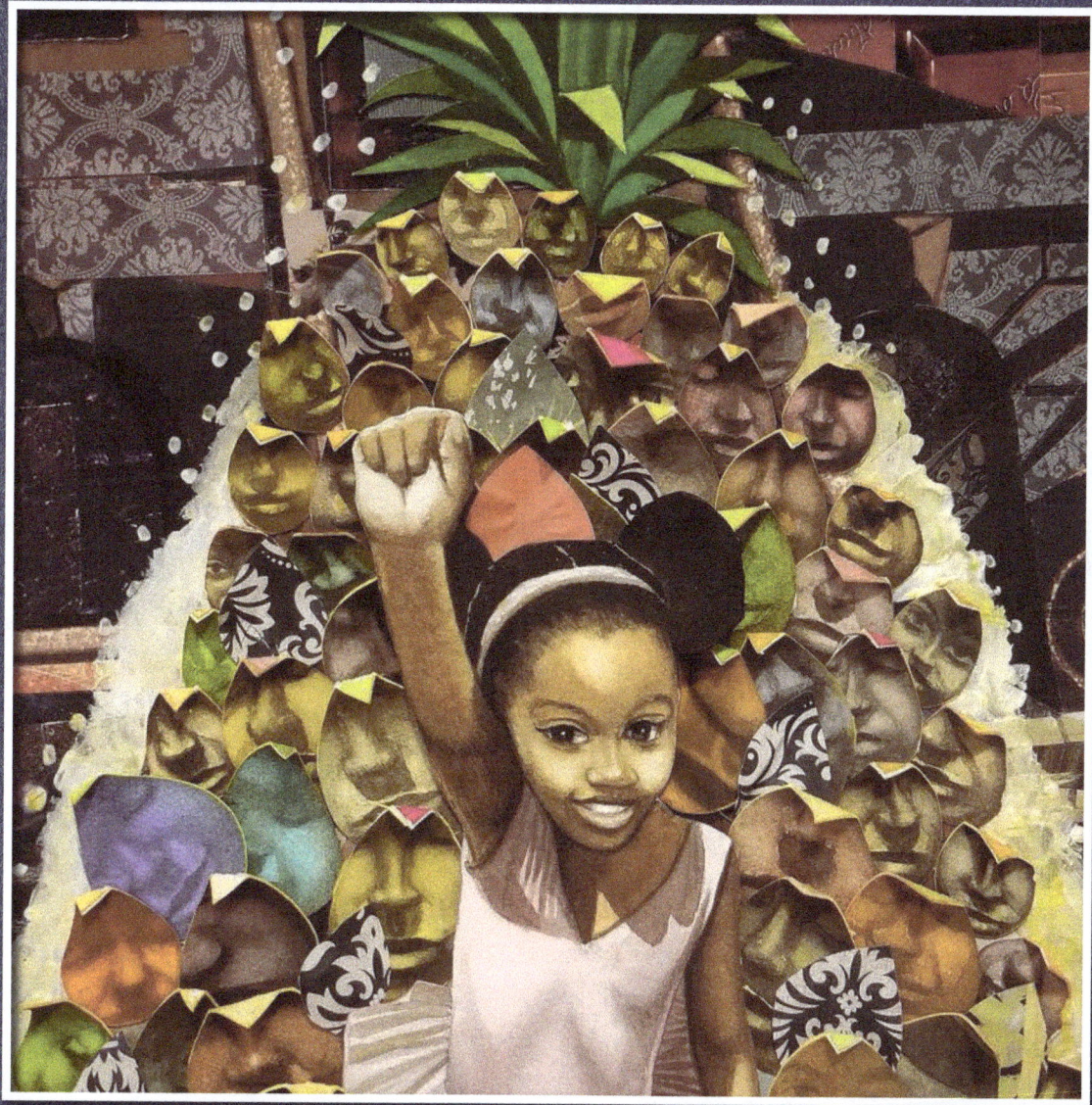

Innocence

To capture innocence

On photographic paper

Is memories delight

It is poetry not written, not drawn...

But

Captured

As you would a soul

All in a child's

Smile

Innocence by camera

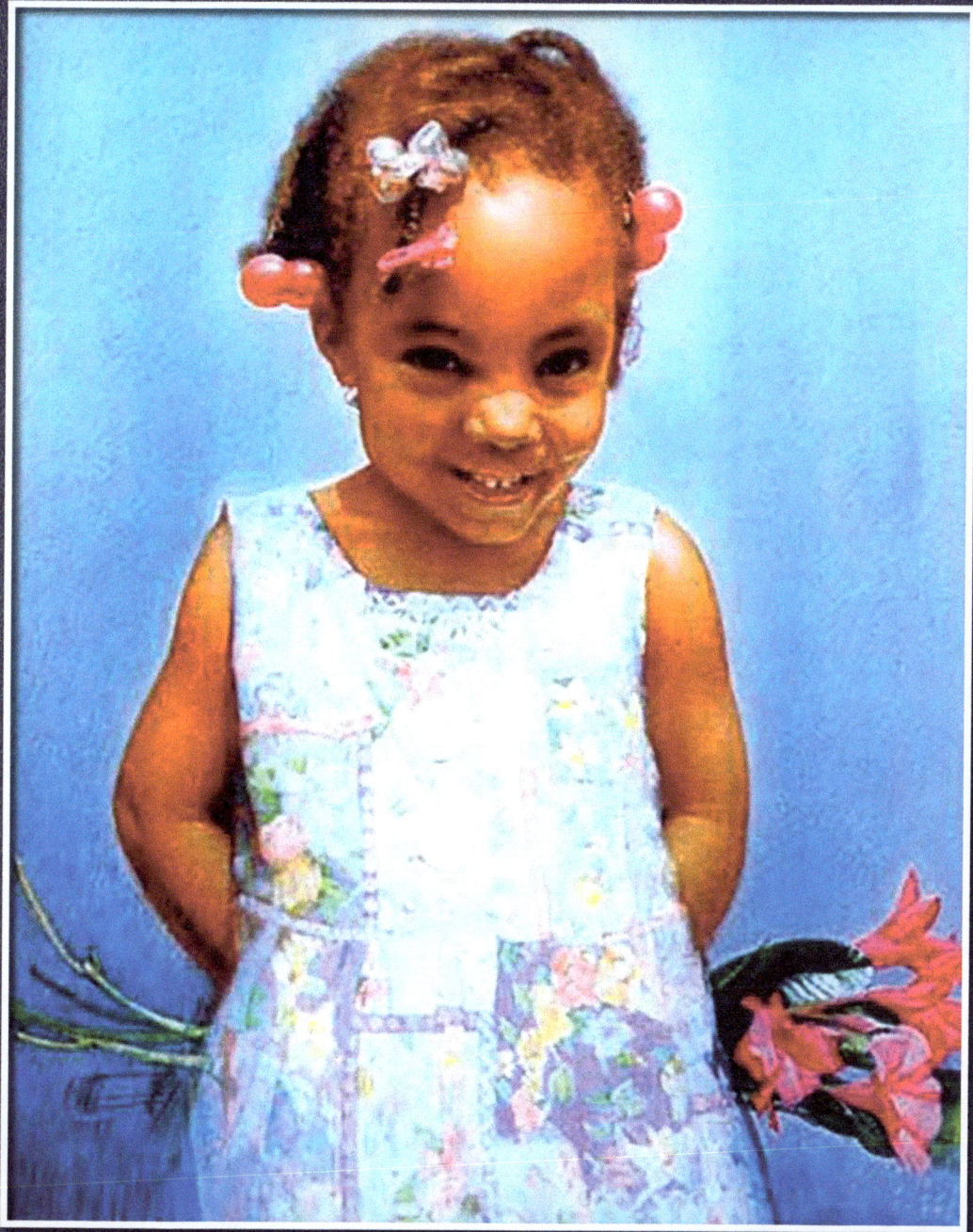

Beauty

It approaches me in the stillness

Of the early morn

And as I appear it darts in to a white cloud, frightened

But lovely still

And I who see stood in awe of creation and its loveliness

Felt anointed by the beauty

The Candle

If I can light a candle in the heart of a little child

And watch it flicker and burn bright

Bright, bright as a morning star

Where all eyes on earth can see

Then and only then

Will I know, I have passed on the light

The love, the passion

In me

One candle to another

Burning bright (merging)

Becoming one

Lighting and caressing the world

To highlight

A gift given so freely

To a little child to fly

Above and beyond the sky...

Memories

There is a Diamond in every memory

Dig for it

As you would

A pearl in the sand...

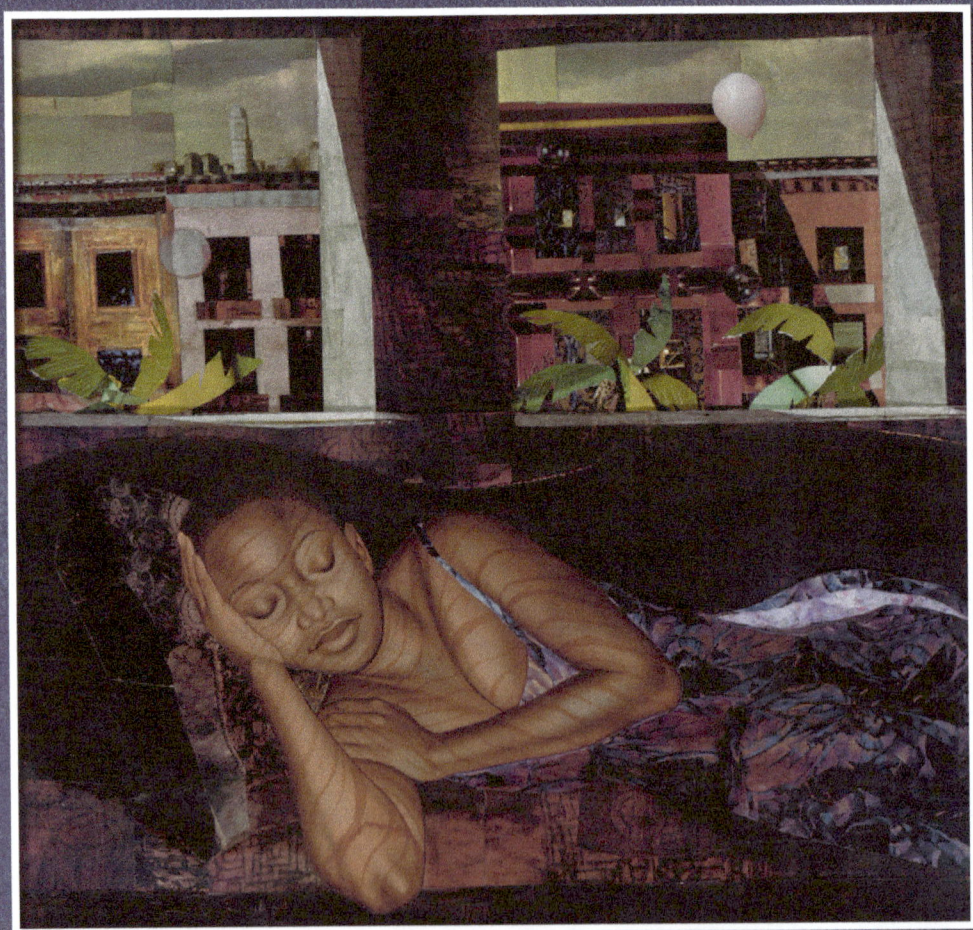

Dreams

Dreams

A dream in your heart is worth a

Thousand...

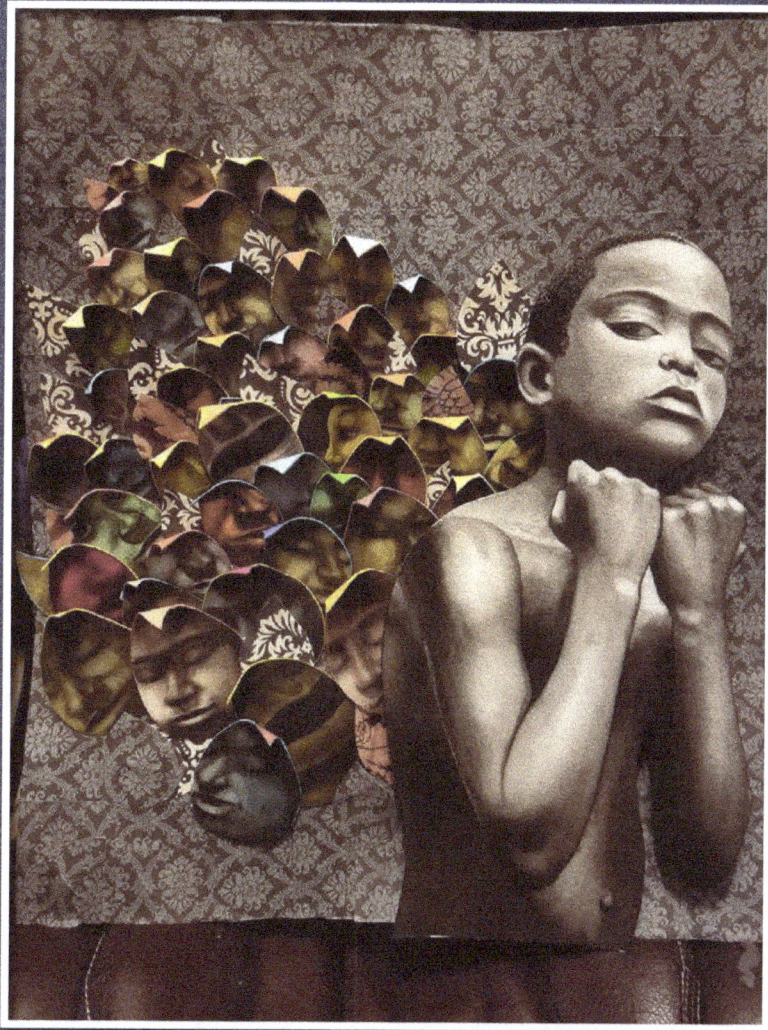

A Thousand Dreams

I have a dream

That one day I will sing a happy song

Little children will march

Hold hands, watch the seagulls

Run in the rain

Together we will write poetry

And make our own music

Build sand castles

Watch the idle moon

Talk to the stars and

Love the lazy nights

And together welcome the long days, to tell stories and

Search for flowers

I have a dream

A thousand dreams

Our dream

A happy song sung

33

A Divine Winter's Dream

Have you ever beheld a winter morning?

With beautiful birds overlooking

A breath-taking waterfall

Where pure living water flows from steps towards you

And suddenly...

Life's cares are lost

In the feathers of a white swan

And all that matters is

This everlasting perfect beauty

Snow-capped mountains

Precious rocks

And a beautiful pearl washed up from the ocean

And then you realize you are lost

In a divine winter's dream

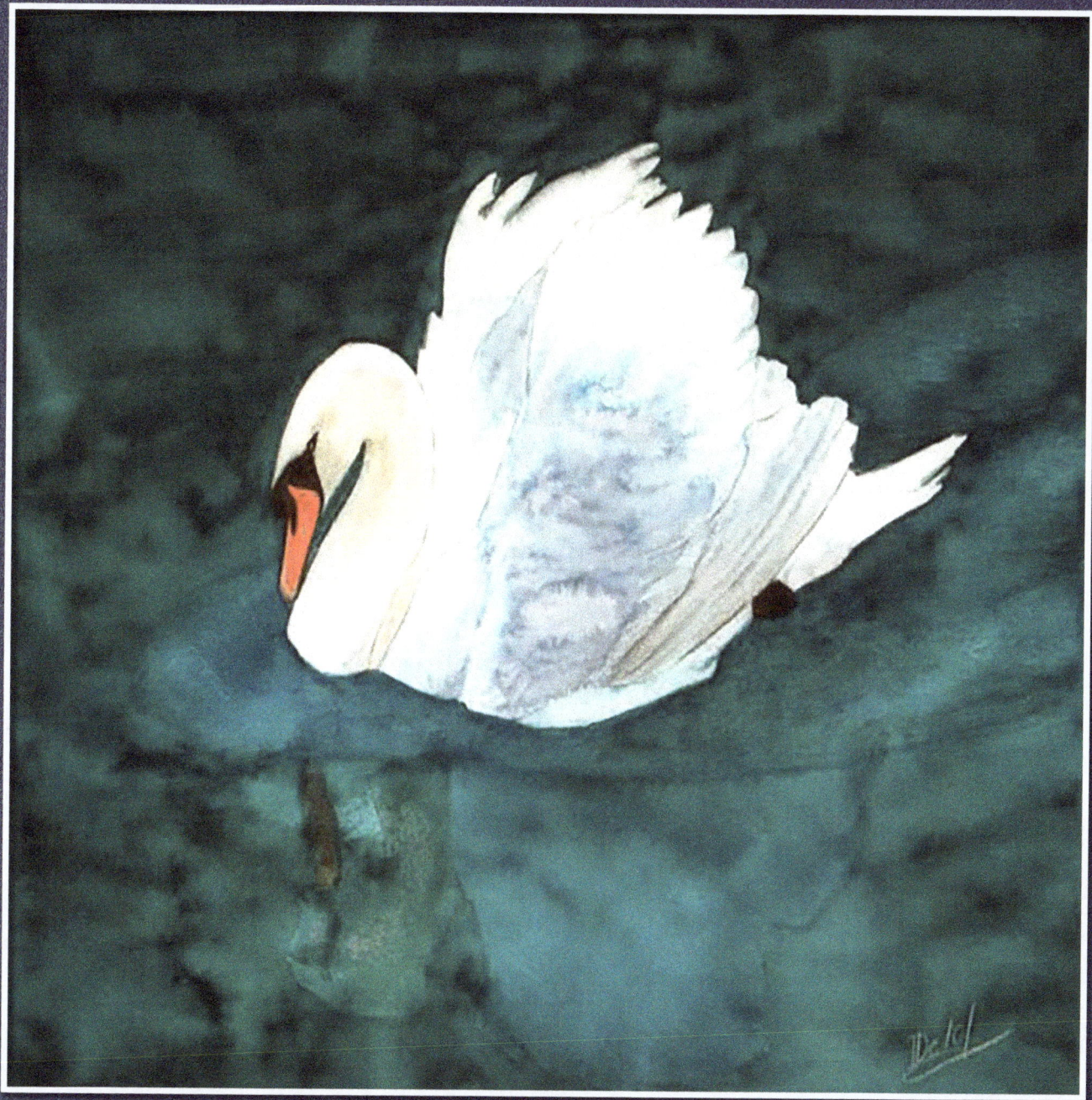

Capture a Dream

Did you ever stop to look at the sky?

This morning

I look up

And a thousand

White dreams

Are there to greet me.

I gather hope

Somehow

I know

It is possible for

Me to capture

A dream...at last

To build a future

Right here

Right now

Right from the sky

The Rainbow

My life is a rainbow

of

quilted children.

Yesterday

Yesterday should have been today

Where I could sit and linger

Ponder

And dream dreams

That

Make life so sweet

So passionate to hold

But today I am back to reality

Facing the real world

Behold I come...

Be a Poet!

Write a poem of your own

Then draw a picture to go with your poem

www.ingramcontent.com/pod-product-compliance
Lightning Source LLC
Chambersburg PA
CBHW041635040426
42448CB00021B/3483